WHAT'S THE BIG IDEA?

A Guide To Creative Marketing Communication

by Jerry Bader

MRP
WEBMEDIA

blurb

Author & Photography: Jerry Bader
Digital Enhancement: Josh Bader
Digital Audio & Sound Design: Simon Bader
Photographic Model: Lindsay Lyon
Video Personality: Cynthia Stone

Preface

AMC ran a series called "The Pitch" that was suppose to be an inside look at the process of how companies hire advertising agencies. On the one hand it was entertaining, and on the other, irritating, a conflict distorted by the process producers deem necessary to create a program that people who are not in the ad business would watch. Like much of television it assumes people are dumb, and although there seems to be adequate anecdotal evidence to support that notion, I do believe that people take what's presented and react accordingly: give them a steady intellectual diet of 'Jersey Shores' and 'Desperate Housewives' and you create an audience of nincompoops; give them 'Breaking Bad' and 'News Room' and you foster intellectual curiosity.

This book is about creativity, and the reason I mention "The Pitch" is that I think the way the agencies were presented makes them look foolish. It trivializes the creative process, and more importantly, the impact creativity can bring to delivering a brand image and marketing message, whether it be for commercial, political, educational, or intellectual purpose.

You may say, so what, who cares about the agencies, they are merely hired hands, artsy plumbers, doing the bidding of their corporate benefactors. The problem is business leaders manage scared, petrified of the public, frightened by the very stuff they sell, and terrified as hell to make a mistake, or that people will find out what's really behind the curtain. The result: airwaves, magazines, and the Internet are crammed with mind numbing advertising based on statistics not human behavior.

'What's The Big Idea?' is a humble attempt to present just one approach to the creative process, a process that is based on human reaction to stimulus rather than statistical analysis, focus groups, or surveys.

What's The Big Idea?
An Organized Approach to Creative Concept Development

How do you generate big ideas and concepts; how do you spark creativity? Everyone in the advertising industry understands that effective marketing starts with big ideas, and ends with persistence and patience. The ad industry has fallen into a malaise fostered by businesses run by MBAs, accountants, and Internet entrepreneurs led astray by a false confidence in numbers and a reliance on technical answers to human problems.

There are those who are creative in a fine art sense where creativity is only limited by talent, imagination and desire, but to be creative for someone else with goals, budgets, and limitations is not an easy way to make a living. It's no wonder there are so many agencies around that follow the numbers, not because the statistics and analytics are so telling, but because they are a hell of a lot easier to sell to a client than an idea that sparks the audience's imagination and delivers emotional impact.

What appears logical and safe often misses the point, and in the end, leads to disappointing results. We live in a 'cover-your-ass' world where most people are content with playing it safe, but effective advertising is the opposite of playing it safe. In the words of advertising great George Lois, the goal of a campaign must be to evoke a response of "Holy Sh*t".

"Advertising, an art, is constantly besieged and compromised by logicians and technocrats, the scientists of our profession who wildly miss the main point about everything we do..."
– George Lois

WHAT'S THE BIG IDEA?

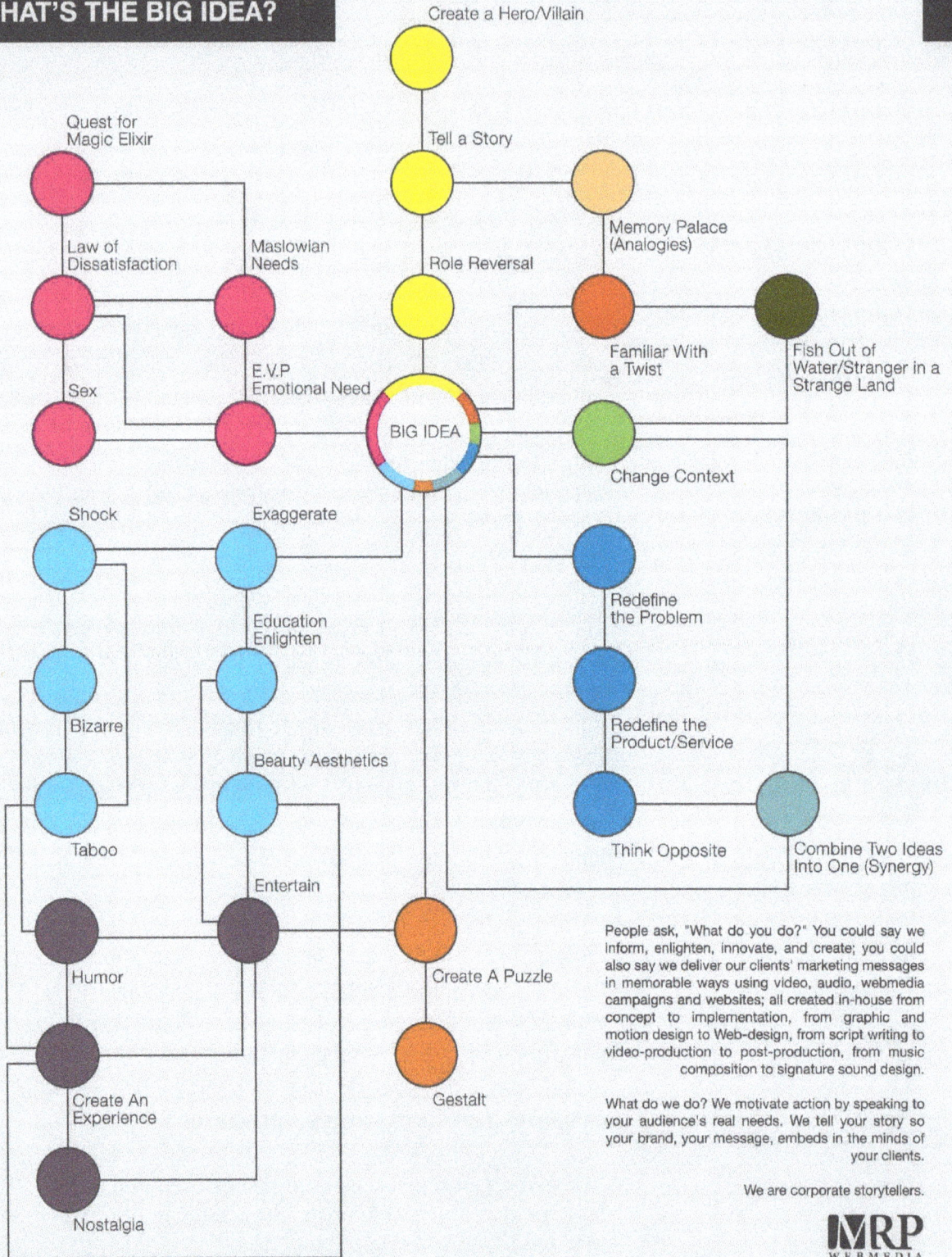

Create a Hero/Villain

Tell a Story

Memory Palace (Analogies)

Quest for Magic Elixir

Role Reversal

Familiar With a Twist

Fish Out of Water/Stranger in a Strange Land

Law of Dissatisfaction

Maslowian Needs

E.V.P Emotional Need

Sex

BIG IDEA

Change Context

Shock

Exaggerate

Redefine the Problem

Education Enlighten

Bizarre

Beauty Aesthetics

Redefine the Product/Service

Taboo

Entertain

Think Opposite

Combine Two Ideas Into One (Synergy)

Humor

Create A Puzzle

Create An Experience

Gestalt

Nostalgia

People ask, "What do you do?" You could say we inform, enlighten, innovate, and create; you could also say we deliver our clients' marketing messages in memorable ways using video, audio, webmedia campaigns and websites; all created in-house from concept to implementation, from graphic and motion design to Web-design, from script writing to video-production to post-production, from music composition to signature sound design.

What do we do? We motivate action by speaking to your audience's real needs. We tell your story so your brand, your message, embeds in the minds of your clients.

We are corporate storytellers.

MRP
WEBMEDIA

Brainstorming Concepts

Brainstorming ideas for a client can of course take on many different approaches depending on the agency, talent, and skill set of the people who work there. But advertising is more than the latest techno-gimmick, fad-app or mobile whiz-bangery; and it's certainly more than just a pretty photograph, illustration, or layout; advertising is psychological persuasion and emotional manipulation, so if you don't bring all the aspects of technical, creative, and psychological know-how together, you're merely wasting your time and money.

Mind Maps

Mind maps have been around for a while, and when you're under the gun for a solution or that blank page is giving you a migraine, then mind maps can come in handy as a way to spark the imagination. According to Wikipedia, "A **mind map** is a diagram used to represent words, ideas, tasks, or other items linked to, and arranged around, a central key word or idea." So if advertising is all about devising a strategy and tactics around a big idea, then mind maps can be a good place to start.

Now you could just sit down and start writing down random thoughts connected to your product or service, and that might work, but chances are you'd end-up writing down all the same things you always think about, leading to the same conclusions and probably the same results. What we're aiming for is something different, a new approach and a reaction that George Lois would approve. The following is a creative development mind map designed to spark creative ideas with an associated explanation of each approach.

Maslowian Needs

Maslow's Hierarchy of Needs provides the advertiser with the ammunition required to turn tire-kickers into buyers. Where on Maslow's list of hardwired primal needs does your product or service rest? Does your offering fulfill physical, safety, social, esteem-related, or self-actualization needs? Most advertising boils down to one of the basic reptilian brain survival strategies: will it kill me, can I eat it, or will it have sex with me? Even the higher rungs of Maslow's pyramid are fundamentally survival strategies that create advantage for those able to compete on an aesthetic or intellectual level.

Emotional Need:
Emotional Value Proposition

Decisions are made in the subconscious as a result of the amygdala's response to some outside stimulus that triggers an emotional reaction. If the emotional reaction is strong enough, your audience will seek out justifications to buy your product. It isn't about logic or features; it's about getting your audience's heart pumping and juices flowing. So what's the emotional value you promise to deliver to your audience?

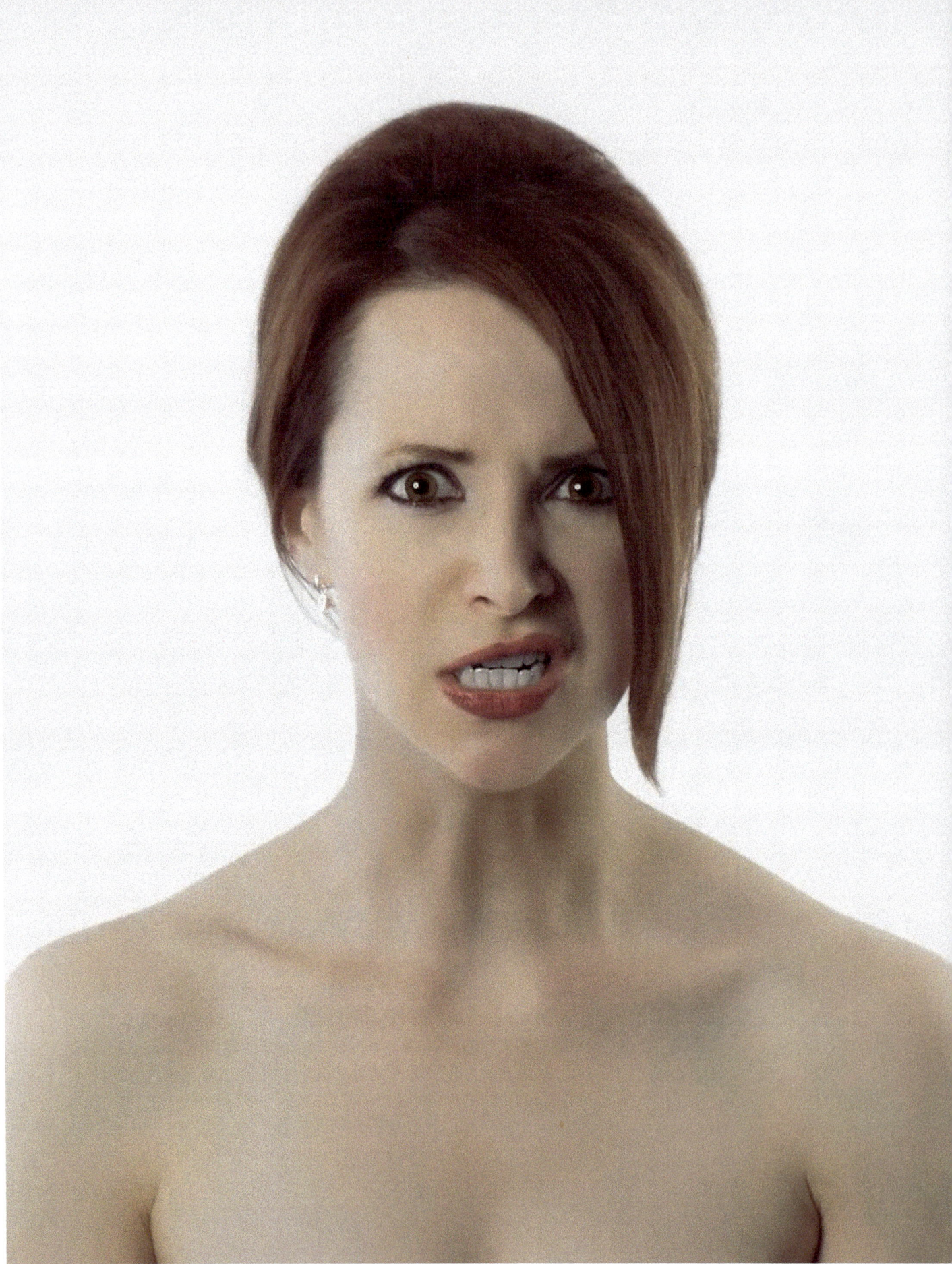

The Law of Dissatisfaction

If you're really, really happy with your spouse, your television, or your cell phone, you don't go out and get a new one. People buy things because they become unhappy with the stuff they've got. If you want to make people happy with the products you sell, you first have to make them unhappy with the stuff they already have. As much as certain cosmetic brands talk about the attractiveness of the natural look, their entire marketing effort is really aimed at telling women, they need something more than what nature has provided.

Quest For The Magic Elixir

Every cosmetic advertisement is based on the notion that there is some magic formula that will convert an ugly duckling into a beautiful swan. Men are not immune to this type of vanity with Axe Body Spray promising to bring a stampeding harem to your front door, or Viagra promising a lifetime of virility. When it comes to one of Maslow's fundamental needs, sex, you can be sure people will be attentive to anything that promises success.

Exaggerate

You have to be careful with this technique. Exaggerating claims that have no basis in reality is definitely a no-no, whereas obvious exaggeration of a scenario for affect can be both memorable and entertaining. The "How it feels to chew 5 gum" TV spots are obvious exaggerations without the need to worry about someone suing Wrigley because each stick of gum didn't actually come with a giant vat of pulsating ball bearings or a warehouse full of blow dryers able to suspend you in mid air.

Shock

Like exaggeration, playing the "shock" card can backfire if you don't handle it correctly. Public service announcements about drinking and driving, or smoking, that emphasize the grisly potential consequences can turn an audience off as often as they can shock viewers to their senses, but shocking or even just amazing your audience can make your viewers sit-up and take notice if handled right.

Federal Express has never matched the impact of their fast talking executive spots featuring actor John Moschitta; the commercials definitely delivered the message that FedEx was the answer to urgent business shipping needs. The audience was shocked, or more accurately amazed, at how fast Moschitta was able to deliver his lines, and the commercials still work years later.

Bizarre

The technique you choose is definitely dependent on your target audience. When it comes to the bizarre, I think the best advice comes from legendary television producer Gary Marshall (Happy Days, Laverne & Shirley) who once said, that it's okay to be "out there" as long as someone else is "out there" with you. Although I believe this to be true, I think most executives are far too cautious and hamper their marketing by opting for timid non-controversial presentations, presentations that lack any memorable element. One example of bizarre advertising is the Skittles, "Harvest The Rainbow" commercial; it definitely falls into the bizarre category, which is perfect for the product's adolescent audience.

Humor

Humor is another tricky but highly effective technique for creating memorable marketing communication. Humor is all about the script, performance, and timing. The problem with some humorous advertising attempts is that they forget to make a point: all effective marketing should state a position; garnering views and likes are worthless without delivering your message. Most humor is based on the vagaries of the human condition, and if you can relate the erratic chaos of modern urban living to your product in a humorous manner, you will connect with your audience on a meaningful level.

One of the best campaigns that used humor was the "Palace of Light" Shredded Wheat Web series; the script, performance, and timing were all perfect in delivering the company's marketing message. It may be difficult to find the videos but if you can track them down, they are definitely worth viewing.

Taboo

It's hard to believe that anything in this anything goes world is taboo, but as society becomes more and more conservative, especially in the sexually repressed, uptight North American marketplace, there is sure to be language, images, life styles, and ideas that will scare away the faint-of-heart. That fear leaves an opening for those who dare to challenge the "Father Knows Best" and "Leave It To Beaver" mindset. The first job of marketing is to get noticed, and touching a forbidden nerve has always been one way to do it.

Create An Experience

When it comes to creating an experience Apple is the master, From the industrial design of their products and packaging, to the look and operation of their stores, to their advertising and marketing, the experience they deliver is engaging, consistent, artful and exciting. Creating an experience is the essence of creating a brand image and corporate identity. Few companies have Apple's resources, but everyone has a website, videos, and blog, and with a little thought, whatever resources you do have can work together to present a unified front with a memorable business personality.

Create A Puzzle

The human race didn't invent the light bulb or put a man on the moon because they couldn't solve puzzles. Seeking out patterns and putting the pieces together to solve a puzzle, a joke, or a managerial conundrum is what we do, and it's how we remember things so that the next time a similar situation or circumstance comes up we can fast-forward to the answer, even if it's only what detergent to buy. Leaving something to the imagination triggers the need to work out an answer. It's a holistic, Gestalt approach (relating to or concerned with wholes or complete systems rather than with the analysis, treatment, or dissection of parts).

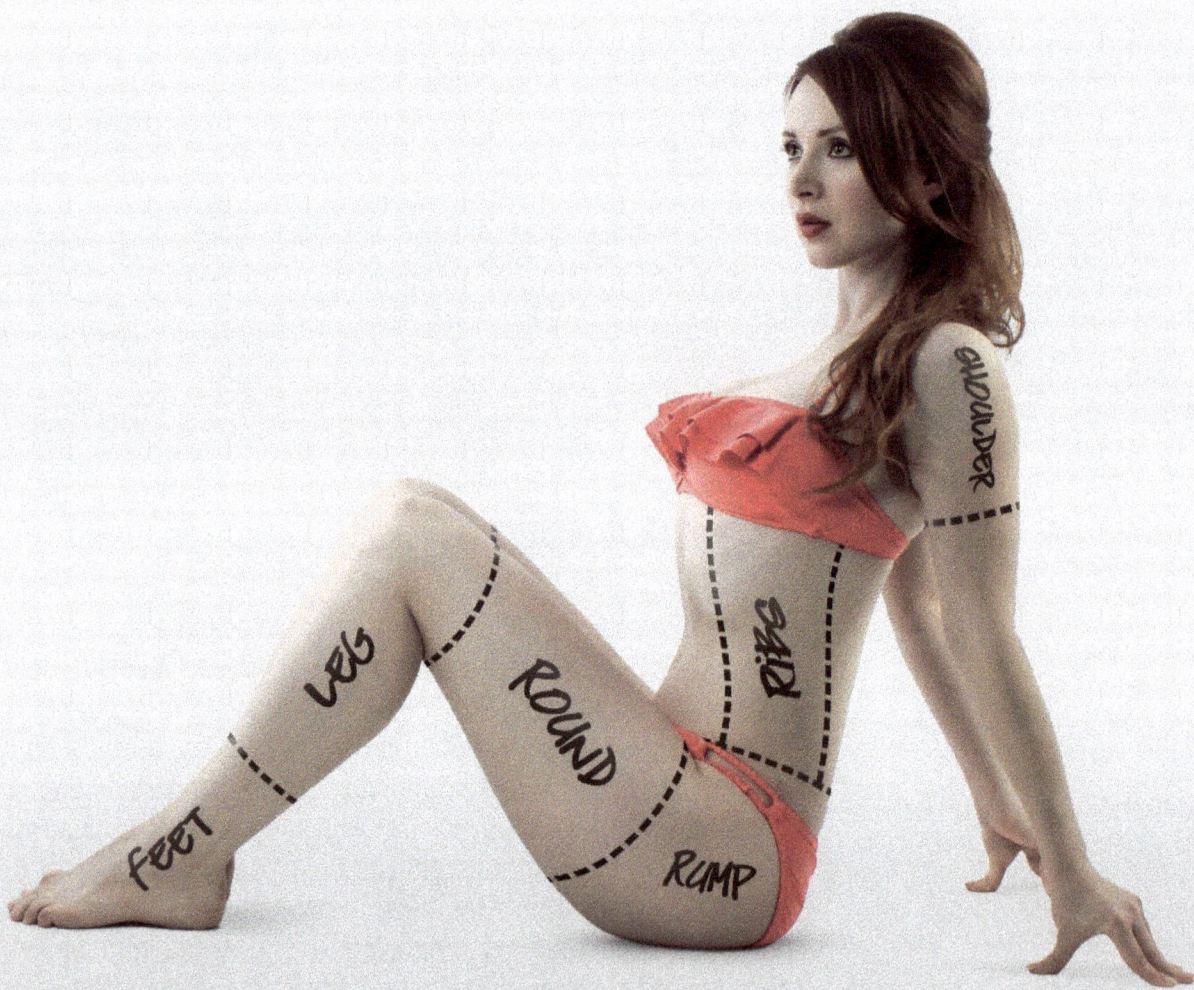

Gestalt

Gestalt: "The principle maintains that the human eye sees objects in their entirety before perceiving their individual parts."
— Wikipedia.

By using Gestalt presentation techniques like Proximity, Similarity, Continuity, Symmetry, Closure, and Common Fate Consequence, we can get an audience to understand and remember the message we want to deliver.

Perhaps you've seen those experiments where a paragraph has been written with all the vowels removed and you can still read it. Our brains automatically solve puzzles, often without us ever realizing what we are dealing with is a riddle, which is why typos often never get caught or corrected. The human brain looks for patterns and meaning, and by forcing your audience to use their brains to interpret your message, you engage their subconscious and imbed your point.

Create Synergy:
Combine Two Ideas Into One

Sometimes big ideas start off as half of an idea. Something is lacking. It can be very frustrating to have half of a great concept, the germ of something special that cannot be implemented because something is missing. Often the answer lies in combining it with another almost good idea, together making something special. If one of these concepts just doesn't seem to deliver enough impact, add another, and together something completely new and special will be created.

Tell A Story

If you don't have a story to tell, you don't have a marketing or advertising strategy. Telling stories is what business communication is all about. The company that tells the most compelling story will beat the competitor that emphasizes price and features every time. Take some time and visit 'The J. Peterman Company' catalogue; click on any product and read the description. Each product has a story to tell, making the product something more than just another dress or jacket.

Entertainment

Advertisers want as many people to see their marketing message as often as possible; television audiences are for the most part captives of their favorite programming, while Web audiences are more selective and can more easily opt-out of marketing messages. As a consequence, website marketing communication has to be on average better than television because companies may only get one shot at delivering the message, and if you only have one chance to make a memorable impression, it better be entertaining.

Create A Hero

Brand heroes are often a good technique for relating to audiences and like all good storytelling the best heroes have their evil opponent. The "I'm A Mac/I'm A PC" television ads are an excellent implementation of this concept without resorting to dressing up an exterminator in a body suit, or bottle of mouthwash in a cape.

There is a lot of discussion around about having a conversation with your public, but much of what is suggested is a misguided implementation of a conceptual notion. By creating a brand hero, you engage your audience and provide them with a context within which they can participate vicariously. This mental participation is the best form of legitimately conversing with your audience in a meaningful manner.

Familiar With A Twist
(The Same But Different)

Back in the day when Hollywood was Hollywood, and studios were film factories with contract players, every studio had their familiar types. Casting was always a question of, "get me a younger, older, sexier, skinnier, etcetera, version of so-and-so." Connecting with an audience has always been a search for the different but familiar.

It's rare that companies actually sell a product or service that is substantially different from the competition in any meaningful way. Most companies sell some variation of something that somebody else sells, so why should they buy yours? A hamburger is a hamburger but a place that sells an 8,000 calorie, artery clogging hamburger meal served by waitresses wearing skimpy nurse's uniforms is different; it's still just a burger, but one that stands out from the competition.

Role Reversal

The news media, before it decided broadcasting real news was too difficult for the audience to grasp and instead chose to fill the airwaves with unsubstantiated gossip, sleazy non relevant scandals, and a substantial helping of political innuendo, spin and demagoguery, used to decide what is, and what is not a news story with a simple concept: dog bites man is NOT news; man bites dog is: it's the reversal-of-roles that makes the audience sit-up and take notice. One of the most famous role-reversal ads was football great, Joe Namath wearing Hanes Beautymist pantyhose. And it is not surprising that it was George Lois, Mr. "Holy Sh*t" himself, who created the ad.

Inform. Educate. Enlighten.

Service is dead. Products are more and more complicated, especially in an era where tech products reign: does anybody know how to get the 12:00 to stop blinking on the stove after the power goes out? Manuals are badly written, often in cryptic or broken English. Most companies can't be bothered with people once they've bought something. This is especially true on the Internet, where people can hide behind contact forms and emails that never get answered, or that generate auto-responded boilerplate that answers nothing and says less. With Web Video, companies can teach their customers how to assemble, use, and get the most out of their purchase, making them more likely to buy more stuff.

Nostalgia

Everything that's old is new again. People generally get stuck in their youth, with their musical tastes formed in their teens and dress style in their early adult years. Everyone craves the good old days, even if the good old days where actually lousy. Sometimes the best way to move forward is to move backward in time. Yesterday's junk is today's collectible, why else would their be at least three or four television shows about straggly scavengers roaming the country for junk they can unload to sentimental victims for a profit. Clothing designers reach deep into their closets for bell-bottoms or Cuban heels in order to put a new spin on an old theme. Could the return of a 3D Speedy Alka-Selzer be far behind? Oh wait, he's already here.

Sex

The propagation of the species is fundamental to mankind's survival. As a consequence much of our behavior is aimed at attracting the opposite sex, and this of course applies to women as well as men. The clothes we wear, the cars we drive, and most of the products we buy are intended to make us look better, appear more prosperous, seem more intelligent, and generally be more attractive to a potential mate. No amount of religious, prudish conservatism can change the fact that sex drives much of what we do and why we do it. There is just no denying that sex sells.

Think Opposite

Thinking opposite is a great way to generate a new idea on what has become a stale product or service that lacks pizzazz or trust. E-trade uses a smart-aleck talking baby in their ads as opposed to some avuncular grey-haired executive, a classic case of thinking opposite; this is especially effective today since the blue-suits on Wall Street have lost their credibility. And of course the success of Apple Computer today can be traced back to Steve Job's persistence on following his unique contrarian approach to conventional corporate bureaucratic protocol and decision-making.

Redefine The Problem

Reis and Trout in their book "The 22 Immutable Laws of Marketing" state that if you can't be number one in your category, invent a new category, which is another way of saying, if you can't fix the problem, redefine it. It's the classic example of why the railroads declined when they were met with alternative forms of transportation (trucking, automobile and air) after dominating the market. Railroads always saw themselves as merely railroads, whereas their competition redefined themselves as transportation companies. Today the industry has redubbed itself "logistics" to better describe the integration of services.

Redefine The Product or Service

I was never one to buy into the idea that customers are always right, but sometimes they become the MacGyvers of big idea thinking. Clients often invent new ways to use products that have too much competition or too limited a market for the originally intended purpose.

If marketing people could remove the blinkers, they too might be able to benefit from a redefinition strategy. Water Displacement-40th Attempt, otherwise known as WD-40, was originally developed to displace and repel standing water to prevent corrosion in nuclear missiles. Rogaine, the hair growing treatment, was originally developed as a drug to treat high blood pressure, and Play-Doh, the kid's modeling compound, was originally developed in the 1930s as a wallpaper cleaner.

Change The Context

Changing context is similar to redefining purpose, but with special attention paid to environment, circumstance, and demographic. A rather obscure product, Bag Balm, was originally developed in the 1800s as a farm product used to sooth milking cows' udders, but the unintended consequence of use was that it also softened the farmers' hands; softening hands (a beauty context) has a far greater market potential with a far higher profit margin than soothing udders (a farm context), so take the product out of the farmer's shed and place it in a woman's beauty kit.

Fish Out of Water
Stranger In A Strange Land

In the 1960s Red Rose Tea ran a commercial using a Zoot-suited jazz band of chimpanzees complete with a scat-singing chimp bandleader singing the company's jingle. It's one of the most memorable TV spots ever made. In 2006 CareerBuilder used a similar scenario: they placed a befuddled regular guy in an environment of wild partying chimpanzee office workers, the result was hilarious and absolutely memorable. When stuck for an idea think "Planet of the Apes," Charlton Heston was a stranger in a strange land.

Memory Palace

If you want your audience to remember who you are, what you do, and why they should care, you have to paint them a picture. If you wrap your offering in an analogy you will stimulate their senses and trigger their emotions, and provide a memorable experience. A Memory Palace is a memory trick that associates one thing with another so that the first thing is easier to remember.

If you can never remember the actor Kevin Spacey's name but you know he was in a movie (K-Pax) where he played a delusional psychiatric patient who thinks he's a spaceman, therefore Spaceman-Spacey; it's an easy and effective method, especially for Web Video marketing that relies on impact rather than repetition like broadcast forms of marketing.

Beauty Aesthetics

Corporate executives tend to be tall and handsome. Attractive people have a definite advantage in all kinds of situations. There is just no denying that beauty and aesthetics count; it is hard-wired into our DNA as a selection criteria. Survival of the fittest is in part survival of the pretty; uniform features are interpreted as good breeding stock; and no one searches for the Fountain of Ugly.

Even on a more sophisticated level, aesthetics carry weight: once people have achieved their basic needs, they strive for something greater, something that approaches perfection, and even if they can't attain it themselves, they'll attempt to associate themselves with things that do: even the nerd can buy an iPhone and a plain Jane can shop at Victoria's Secret.

Finally

"A quality of great art is its ability to guide attention from one of its parts to another in a manner that pleasures, informs, and provokes."

– E. O. Wilson, 'The Social Conquest'

Advertising like art is not a place for statistical buffoonery but rather the realm of creative minds. Where the number crunchers brought us derivatives and financial ruin, people like George Lois brought smiles to our faces and new customers to clients. Whether it's Norman Rockwell's comfort-paintings for Coca Cola or Helmut Newton's libido pulsing fashion photography, marketing is an art form and like all great art the best "guides attention… in a manner that pleasures, informs, and provokes."

Postscript

Perhaps you're still not convinced that creativity is the key to developing a big idea that can be used as the basis for business success, in which case consider the following observations.

The Advertising Research Foundation ran an advertising experiment to test the noise factor involved in display ad click-through rates. In other words, what portion of click-throughs were meaningless impulse and random curiosity? Ted McConnell, ARF's Executive VP-Digital, was intrigued by a friend's comment that any time he wanted to pump-up his clicks and make some "quick money" he'd "buy late-night impressions on women's gaming sites". It seems this audience would, from boredom, random curiosity, or just plain the hell-of-it, click on just about anything. In which case, one has to ask, does the current obsession with targeting supposed statistically relevant demographic profiles and the subsequent premium companies pay for access to such analytic manipulation really impact click-through results?

So to test the validity of market segmentation, ARF created a series of blank ads in various standard sizes, in two colors, white and orange. "The average click-through rate across half a million ads served was 0.08%, which would be good for a brand campaign, and so-so for a direct response campaign." - How Blank Display Ads Managed to Tot Up Some Impressive Numbers, Ted McConnell

Considering the impressive results of a blank, meaningless, message-less ad, one has to wonder why anyone would pay for marketing systems based on what appears to be faulty assumptions. Perhaps Seinfeld was correct: stuff about nothing has as much audience draw as stuff about something, or was there something else going when people clicked on blank colored boxes?

Which leads me to my second observation, and that is the importance of I-R Theory in creating effective, memorable marketing communication. I-R Theory or Incongruity-Resolution Theory basically states that humor producing laughter and memory results from the 'aha moment' created by the brain's resolution of the incongruities and inconsistencies between our assumptions and reality.

Because we are hardwired to look for patterns of behavior in order to make quick decisive decisions, a survival mechanism, we often make false assumptions. Humor, drama, story telling, and creativity in general are all based on the tension created by building assumption-filled scenarios and allowing the audience to resolve the conflicts between those assumptions and reality, thereby releasing the tension and providing a feeling of accomplishment and success. The reaction to solving a riddle creates a powerful memory that in business terms is the goal of all marketing communication. And perhaps just as importantly, the resolution of incongruities creates a kind of link or bond between the viewer and advertiser, a shared "I get it" moment that creates a kind of social glue. The act of clicking on a blank colored square comes from the human need to solve an incongruity, or in other words, create a riddle and people will need to solve it.

Creativity is the key to developing big ideas that work. An over reliance on the false assumptions taken from statistical manipulation, fad marketing, and technical solutions to human problems will only inhibit the process of connecting to your audience.

"When I examine myself and my methods of thought, I come close to the conclusion that the gift of imagination has meant more to me than any talent for absorbing absolute knowledge... I feel certain I am right while not knowing the reason."

– Einstein

About The Author

Jerry Bader is Senior Partner at MRPwebmedia, a media production and design firm that specializes in delivering clients' marketing messages in memorable ways using video, audio, webmedia campaigns and websites; all created in-house from concept to implementation, from graphic and motion design to Web-design, from script writing to video-production to post-production, from music composition to signature sound design. MRPwebmedia turns advertising into content, and content into a memorable experience.

MRPwebmedia.com
(905) 764-1246
info@mrpwebmedia.com

About MRPwebmedia

People ask, "What do you do?" You could say we inform, enlighten, innovate, and create; you could also say we deliver our clients' marketing messages in memorable ways using video, audio, webmedia campaigns and websites; all created in-house from concept to implementation, from graphic and motion design to Web-design, from script writing to video-production to post-production, from music composition to signature sound design.

What do we do? We motivate action by speaking to your audience's real needs. We tell your story so your brand, your message, embeds in the minds of your clients. We are corporate storytellers; we turn advertising into content, and content into a memorable experience.

A Contrarian's Perspective

The Internet is the most democratic communication platform ever created, but democracy is messy. Everyone has a chance to contribute, but the downside is along side the good stuff, is a lot of confused analysis, misguided technical crazes, and pop culture fads misrepresented as legitimate trends.

The glut of misunderstood media hype has had an undue influence on marketing plans, wasting valuable time and money. Marketing is, and always has been, the art of creative thinking and presentation; a perspective that has been compromised by a business climate that fosters a cover-your-ass mindset, resulting in a cabal of number crunchers calling the creative shots. "What's The Big Idea?" presents an alternative point-of-view for those willing to put aside technical obsession and statistical manipulations, and create a marketing strategy based on human nature.

Jerry Bader,
Senior Partner, MRPwebmedia.com

MRP
WEBMEDIA